BUILDING

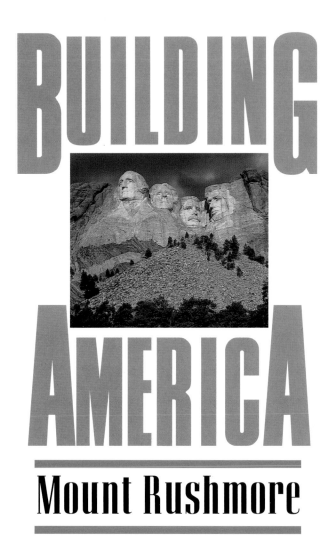

AMERICA

Mount Rushmore

Craig A. Doherty and Katherine M. Doherty

A BLACKBIRCH PRESS BOOK

WOODBRIDGE, CONNECTICUT

Special Thanks

The authors wish to thank the many librarians who helped them find the research materials for this series—especially Donna Campbell, Barbara Barbieri, Yvonne Thomas, and the librarians at the New Hampshire State Library.

The publisher would like to thank James G. Popovich, of the National Park Service, and the South Dakota Department of Tourism for their valuable help in putting this book together.

Published by Blackbirch Press, Inc.
One Bradley Road
Woodbridge, CT 06525

© 1995 Blackbirch Press, Inc.
First Edition

Printed in Hong Kong

10 9 8 7 6 5 4 3 2 1

Photo Credits

Cover: Courtesy Mount Rushmore National Memorial/National Park Service, U.S. Department of the Interior.

Pages 4, 6, 8 (top), 10, 11, 13, 16, 19, 20, 21, 23, 24, 26, 28–32, 34, 36, 40, 42–43: courtesy Mount Rushmore National Memorial/National Park Service, U.S. Department of the Interior; page 9 (Washington and Lincoln): National Portrait Gallery; page 9 (Jefferson): Library of Congress; page 12: National Portrait Gallery; page 14: Library of Congress; page 27: George Faasbeder, Black Hills Studios/courtesy Mount Rushmore National Memorial; page 38: courtesy South Dakota Department of Tourism; page 39: courtesy Crazy Horse Archives.

Library of Congress Cataloging-in-Publication Data

Doherty, Katherine M.
    Mount Rushmore / by Katherine M. Doherty and Craig A. Doherty.—1st ed.
        p. cm.—(Building America)
    Includes bibliographical references and index.
    ISBN 1-56711-108-4
    1. Borglum, Gutzon, 1867-1941—Juvenile literature. 2. Mount Rushmore National Memorial (S.D.)—Juvenile literature.
    [1. Borglum, Gutzon, 1867-1941. 2. Mount Rushmore National Memorial (S.D.)
    3. National Memorials.] I. Doherty, Craig A. II. Title. III. Series: Building America (Woodbridge, Conn.)
    NB237.B6D65 1995   94-24757
    730'.92—dc20   CIP
                                                                        AC

Table of Contents

INTRODUCTION...5

CHAPTER 1   In Search of the Right Mountain...7

CHAPTER 2   Carved in Stone...........................17

CHAPTER 3   One President at a Time...............25

CHAPTER 4   The Finishing Touches.................33

CHAPTER 5   A Memorial for Millions..............37

GLOSSARY..44
CHRONOLOGY..45
FURTHER READING...46
SOURCE NOTES..46
INDEX...47

Introduction

It took 14 years to blast and chisel almost half a million tons of granite from the cliff of Mount Rushmore, in South Dakota. All this work, however, created the 60-foot-tall faces of Presidents George Washington, Thomas Jefferson, Abraham Lincoln, and Theodore Roosevelt. From the start, it was a project surrounded by controversy.

Originally, the idea of such a memorial was proposed by Doane Robinson, the secretary and historian of the South Dakota Historical Society in 1924. He thought a sculpture of heroic westerners would be a good way to attract tourists to South Dakota. Robinson knew of one sculptor in particular who he thought would be right for the job: a man named Gutzon Borglum.

When Robinson wrote to Borglum in 1924, the sculptor had already completed a number of well-known works. He had also recently left a similar project at Stone Mountain, Georgia. For Borglum, the offer came at a good time. He and his son, Lincoln, traveled to South Dakota to talk to Robinson and scout possible sites. After a long search, Borglum finally found a location suitable for the grand project. By 1927, the Black Hills were ringing with the sound of drills and the blasting of dynamite.

In Search of the Right Mountain

The Black Hills are situated in the southwest corner of South Dakota, and they have long played a unique role in the history of the area. Geologically speaking, they are some of the oldest mountains in the world, with prehistoric granite domes formed from hot, liquid magma over 1.5 billion years ago. The granite outcroppings that are formed throughout the area seemed to offer the perfect material for the type of sculpture Borglum and Robinson envisioned.

The decision to create a memorial in the Black Hills was not without controversy. Many editorials in the papers of South Dakota spoke out against the

Opposite:
The Mount Rushmore memorial is carved from the granite of the Black Hills in South Dakota.

idea. Some said that the natural beauty of the area would be destroyed, while others said no one would ever travel all the way to South Dakota just to see some faces carved in rock. Robinson and Borglum, however, paid little attention to the clatter of negative publicity and proceeded with their ambitious and rather unique plan.

In the summer of 1925, Borglum toured the Harney Range of the Black Hills with Theodore Shoemaker, the South Dakota state forester, in search of the right location to place the memorial. Borglum had a number of conditions he hoped would be met by the site: First and foremost, he wanted the site to be big enough for the grand scale he envisioned. Second, the rock needed to be tightly grained and void of any obvious flaws, like cracks or changes in the quality of the stone. And lastly, he hoped the area would face south to capture the sun throughout the day.

After seeing and climbing many of the granite outcroppings of the Harney Range, Borglum chose the impressive rock at Mount Rushmore. The face of the rock was big enough—400 feet high and 1,000

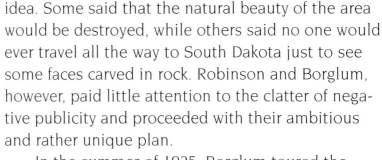

A view of the rock at Mount Rushmore in 1925, before the memorial was carved.

feet long—the granite seemed solid and tightly grained, and the mountain faced in a southeasterly direction.

Whose Faces to Carve?

Before, during, and after the creation of the memorial, the final decision of whose faces were to be carved created a major controversy. Robinson thought Mount Rushmore should honor western heroes like Lewis and Clark, John Fremont, and James Bridger. Borglum, however, felt that if the memorial was going to attract tourists from all over the country, the subjects needed to be better-known national statesmen.

In the end, the task of picking the subjects was left to Borglum to decide, and he chose four of America's most popular presidents. George Washington, as the first president of the United States and the most revered political figure in the history of our country, seemed an obvious selection. Thomas Jefferson was the second president chosen. Borglum felt that Jefferson should be included, in part, because of his participation in the founding of the country and especially because it was during Jefferson's presidency that the Louisiana Purchase was made. (Before 1803, France owned the territory west of the Mississippi to the Rocky Mountains. With the Louisiana Purchase, Jefferson acquired this territory for $15 million and doubled the size of the United States.) Abraham Lincoln had already been studied by Borglum, who did the marble bust of the 16th president that sits in the Capitol Rotunda, and a Lincoln bronze for the city of Newark, New Jersey.

Top:
George Washington
Middle:
Thomas Jefferson
Bottom:
Abraham Lincoln

JOHN GUTZON DE LA MOTHE BORGLUM

Although the name John Gutzon de la Mothe Borglum may not be familiar to most, there are very few people who do not know this sculptor's most famous work—Mount Rushmore. Gutzon Borglum, as he was known, was born on March 25, 1867, in Idaho territory, to Jens Borglum and Christina Mikkelson Borglum. Jens Borglum had come to the United States from Denmark in part because he joined the Mormon Church. When Jens first arrived in America, he married Ida Mikkelson. When her sister Christina arrived a few years later, all three were joined in marriage, which was a common practice among Mormons of the time.

The growing Borglum family moved around the West, and when Gutzon was four, the three-way marriage broke up. Christina, Gutzon's mother, left her sister, Jens, and her two sons. At this point, the family moved to St. Louis, Missouri, where Jens hid the fact that, at one time, he had two wives and children born by both wives. This "family secret" was

Gutzon Borglum raises the American flag during the mountain's dedication in 1925.

one that Gutzon Borglum kept even as an adult. Some who have studied his life suggest that part of his trouble in dealing with people as an adult may have been a result of the unhappiness he felt about being brought up by his aunt and never being allowed to see his biological mother again.

Borglum left home at the age of 17 and moved to California, where his passion for art first came to public attention. Teaching art, painting portraits and western landscapes, were all activities he pursued during the five years he spent in California. In 1889, at the age of 22, Borglum married his art instructor, Lisa Putnam, a 40-year-old widow. Together, they went to Europe to further pursue his career in art.

While in Europe, Borglum befriended and studied under the famous French sculptor, Auguste Rodin, whose best-known sculpture is called "The Thinker." It was in the art of sculpture that Borglum was to find his life's love. For the next nine years, his career went very well, and he received a number of commissions for sculptures both in Europe and the United States. His marriage, however, did not survive, and he was divorced in 1908.

Within a year, Borglum remarried, this time to Mary Montgomery. He had two children with his second wife: James Lincoln Borglum—born in 1912—and

Sculptor Borglum at work in 1930

Mary Ellis Borglum—born in 1916. Borglum continued to have success as a sculptor, and although his work was not always critically acclaimed, it was well received by most people who liked his naturalistic style.

Borglum's better-known works include some of the figures on the Cathedral of Saint John in New York City, the 6-ton marble bust of Abraham Lincoln that sits in the Rotunda of the U.S. Capitol building, and a bronze statue of U.S. General Philip H. Sheridan. Borglum was also the sculptor first commissioned, in 1915, to do the massive sculpture of the leaders of the Confederacy on Stone Mountain in Georgia.

The Stone Mountain project ended in disaster for Borglum. He became involved in an argument with the head of the Stone Mountain Association about who had the final word on the artistic aspects of the sculpture.

Many other people who knew Borglum and worked with him considered the artist to be a difficult personality. His antisocial tendencies were shown in a number of ways. One obvious way was his active membership in the Klu Klux Klan, a secretive and openly racist organization. The Klan supported Borglum's work at Stone Mountain, but his argument with the director ended in the sculptor's firing. As soon as he knew he had been let go, he destroyed all his working models so that no one else could use his creations. The memorial remained unfinished for nearly 50 years.

The Stone Mountain Association tried to have Borglum arrested, but he was able to leave Georgia before they caught him. The hard feelings between Georgia and Borglum lasted a long time, and a number of people connected with the Stone Mountain project tried to block his hiring for Mount Rushmore. Fortunately, those people were unsuccessful.

Borglum greatly admired Abraham Lincoln for his determination to keep the country together during the devastating Civil War (1861-1865). Theodore Roosevelt was the most controversial selection that Borglum made, especially since the 26th president had only been dead for six years. Borglum had known Roosevelt when Roosevelt was police commissioner in New York City. Borglum admired his toughness as a political leader. Also, Roosevelt had a ranch in South Dakota, which gave him a special connection to the area. Borglum believed that the completion of the Panama Canal during Roosevelt's presidency connected him to the theme of nation-builders, an idea that Borglum felt the other three men also represented. Since Borglum's subjects were chosen, there have been suggestions for additions to the sculpture. Suggestions have ranged from requests to add President John F. Kennedy to not–so–serious attempts to have a likeness of Elvis Presley carved next to the other great Americans.

Theodore Roosevelt

Money, Money, Money

The greatest challenge faced by Robinson, Borglum, and others associated with the project was coming up with the money to keep the work going. The total amount of time spent actually working on the memorial was only six-and-a-half years. But, due to the lack of funds, the work stopped many times over a period of 14 years before the project was complete. Although Borglum had many rich and influential friends, contributions were very slow in coming. The site's isolation, Borglum's technical problems with his Stone Mountain project, and the controversy that surrounded the selection of the subjects, all contributed to people's reluctance to donate money.

On August 10, 1927, President Calvin Coolidge came to Mount Rushmore and officially dedicated the memorial as Borglum did the ceremonial first drilling up on the mountain. The publicity that surrounded the Coolidge visit gave the fundraising a boost. Enough money was raised to keep people working into early December, when work stopped for the first of many times.

President Calvin Coolidge addresses the crowd during a ceremony that officially marked the beginning of work on the memorial in 1927.

WHOSE HILLS ARE THEY?

The history of the Black Hills has been written with the blood of Sioux Indians. For the Sioux, the Black Hills, which they call *Paha Sapa*, is the center of their spiritual world. It was in these hills that they believed the world was created, and it was here that their spirits and the spirits of their ancestors traveled after death. Traditionally a young Sioux warrior approaching adulthood would venture into the area alone on a vision quest, or special spiritual journey. He traveled in hopes that the vision would guide his way in life. This sacred region, however, was stolen from the Sioux in one of the U.S. Army's blackest campaigns.

On August 24, 1874, a Chicago paper announced that gold had been discovered in the Black Hills. There was a depression in the United States at the time, and thousands of unemployed hopefuls rushed to the Black Hills in search of their fortune. The Black Hills had been promised to the Sioux in a recent peace treaty and was supposed to be off limits to whites. The U.S. government tried to buy the area from the Sioux, but the two sides could not come to an agreement. The government decided they had only one choice: they declared war on the Sioux. After being defeated by the Sioux at Little Big Horn in 1876, the U.S. Army brutally destroyed Sioux territory and forced the remaining Sioux onto reservations.

To many Sioux, the creation of a national memorial that stood for the power and spirit of the United States on their sacred ground was yet another insult added to what seemed an already endless list.

A Sioux medicine man

Because Mount Rushmore was on both federal and state land, laws had been passed in Washington, D.C., and South Dakota authorizing the memorial's construction. No money, however, was granted. With little money coming in and very little progress being made, Senator Peter Norbeck of South Dakota, took a personal interest in the project. As one of Rushmore's major supporters, Norbeck worked with South Dakota representative William Williamson to get a law passed in 1929 that helped the money situation. In addition to helping with money, the law stipulated that no fee could ever be charged to visitors of the memorial, and that has held true to this day.

A new commission, the Mount Rushmore National Memorial Commission, was formed and appointed by President Coolidge. The law granted the commission $250,000 in matching funds. This law was retroactive (applied to a time in the past) and the commission received $55,000 immediately to match the money already spent on the project. If not for Norbeck and Williamson, work on the memorial might have never resumed. Borglum returned to Mount Rushmore and the project started up again in June 1929.

The Great Depression that ravaged the economy of the United States starting in October 1929, contributed to the fundraising problems of Borglum and the commission. At the same time, however, the Depression and the programs of President Franklin D. Roosevelt actually saved the memorial by providing money in various ways until the project was finished. In the end, the memorial cost a total of $989,992— the largest portion paid by the federal government.

2

Carved in Stone

The actual work on the granite mountain was both slow and hard. For Borglum, it required the skills of a hard-rock miner as well as those of an artist. Borglum began the project by creating a working plaster model at his studio, which was located at the base of Mount Rushmore. The model was sculpted on a 1-to-12 scale—that meant 1 inch on the model would equal 12 inches on the mountain. Borglum's 5-foot-high plaster models would translate into 60-foot-tall carvings. When a face shape began to be roughed out on the model, Borglum would extend a

Opposite:
This final version of Borglum's plaster model was used to transfer measurements to the site. Design changes and poor quality rock caused the model to be redone nine times during the memorial's creation.

17

beam straight out from the top of the head and drop a line with a plumb bob (weight that causes the line to hang straight) on its end. Next, the beam would be rotated, and very exact measurements would be taken and then transferred from the models to the mountain.

To get the measurements as exact as possible, a replica of the model, called a sectional mold, was made of each head and brought to the top of the mountain. There, each head could be checked by "the pointers" as they transferred the measurement points from the model to the stone.

Borglum originally made the models in one piece, as he expected them to appear on the cliff face. Problems with the rock, however, forced him to rethink the position of the heads many times. Because of problems in the granite, he had to change his model nine different times, repositioning the heads and adjusting his design.

On the mountain itself, ninety percent of the stone removal process was considered simply a matter of engineering. The final ten percent, however, needed the watchful eye of the artist. Borglum saw the mountain like other artists see a piece of paper or a canvas. Because of this, he did not set out simply to copy the models onto the rock. During the process, he often viewed the mountain from different angles and in different weather and light conditions. After he considered the problems, he would then instruct the workers to make subtle changes in the final, finished details of the faces.

The many men who drilled, blasted, pointed, and did the final finish work spent most of their time suspended from the top of the mountain in some way. The drillers, powdermen, and the workers who helped them, worked from a special rig that Borglum had developed when he was in charge of the Stone Mountain project. The rig he designed consisted of a thick steel frame covered in leather that a worker would sit on. The seat had two safety straps, which made it impossible to fall out. Once strapped into the rigging, the worker was lowered down the face by a hand winch (pulley), and could easily move about on the sculpture. The workers communicated with the winch operators through a "call boy" who would be positioned on the cliff, where he could see both the workers and the winch house. When a worker signaled that he wanted to be raised or lowered, it was the job of the call boy to yell to the winchman, telling him the number of the cable and whether it was to be raised or lowered.

The workers also used scaffolds of various sizes to work on the memorial. A four-by-four-foot cage held one or two workers at the end of a cable while a four-by-eight-foot platform might have room for three or four workers. For the finish work, workers built staging using eight-foot-long railroad timbers bolted directly to special blocks of rock that were left on the surface.

Top:
Inside the Mount Rushmore winch house
Bottom:
Working in a cage suspended by cables

A Dynamite Job

The majority of the stone removed from Mount Rushmore was blasted off using dynamite. To do this, a series of holes were drilled into the rock using air-powered jackhammers that varied in size from 20 to 60 pounds. Using the largest jackhammer and a well-sharpened bit, a driller could go through about one-and-a-half feet of rock a minute. Usually, though, only an eight or nine-inch-deep hole was needed.

The bits would become dull after penetrating approximately three feet of rock, so they constantly needed to be changed. A worker known as a "steel

A blacksmith sharpens drill bits used by workers on the mountain. Drillers could go through more than 400 bits in a single day.

monkey" was in charge of keeping the drillers supplied with bits. He would carry a bag of different length bits and would be raised and lowered to the drillers, who would keep drilling for four hours at a stretch once they were lowered. The steel monkey placed the dull bits in a bucket that went down to the base of the mountain. There, they were sent to a blacksmith's shop for sharpening. The blacksmiths ground the points and then heat-tempered the bits to harden them. All in all, it took a few hundred sharpened bits a day to keep the drillers going.

Once an area of stone was drilled, a worker called a "powder monkey" would be lowered down to place explosive charges. The amount of dynamite placed in each hole depended on how much rock

ENVIRONMENTAL IMPACT

When the carving at Mount Rushmore was started, there were no laws in place that protected the environment, and little concern was given for protecting the land or various forms of local wildlife. Roads and buildings were built where they were needed, without concern for any impact they might have on the local plants or how they would change the habitats of native animals. Laws were passed at both the state and the federal level authorizing construction without any research on the possible effects the memorial's construction would have on the area. With the exception of a few negative editorials in South Dakota papers, there was no public input into the decision to carve up the giant and majestic rock of Mount Rushmore.

Today, the situation would be very different. The National Environmental Policy Act provides strict guidelines for researching and examining the potential impact on the environment of any project of this size and scope. Also, it would now take five to ten years to go through the process of seeking approval for a memorial like Mount Rushmore. An environmental impact study would have to be done first, and then private individuals would be given the opportunity to comment on the study. Appeals could be made if either side was unhappy with the outcome. Congress, too, would have to formally approve the project. It would cost hundreds of thousands of dollars and the chances are very slim that it would ever be approved.

was to be removed. Explosive charges varied from a few sticks per hole to simple blasting caps, which were used as the workers got close to the finished surface. The powder monkey wired the charges together before the wires were hooked to the top of the mountain. Blasting was done only when all the workers were safely on top of the mountain, usually during lunchtime.

It was the pointer's job to make sure that the rock was marked as to how deep it should be drilled at any given point. The measurements were marked directly on the rock by the pointers to guide the drillers. As they got closer to the finished surface, the holes drilled would become shallower, and, instead of dynamite, the rock would be removed by more mechanical means.

Honeycombing was the main technique used to get close to the finished surface of the stone. To do this, the drillers made a number of shallow holes close together, then the stone between the drilled holes was removed either with a jackhammer or— in some of the most critical areas—by hand with a hammer and a chisel. The final finish on the rock was done with special airhammers called bumpers that left the rock as smooth as poured concrete. Throughout the finishing process, Borglum studied the heads, making small changes until he was satisfied with the final appearance.

A driller "honeycombs" the surface of the rock with an air-powered drill before the layer of stone is cleared with a jackhammer or a chisel.

One President at a Time

George Washington's face was carved out of the side of Mount Rushmore first. On July 4, 1930, a dedication ceremony was held, even though the Washington face was nowhere near complete. The ceremony was held mostly to generate new interest in the project and to stimulate donations needed to keep the work going. More than 2,500 people attended the dedication to see the partially completed face of Washington unveiled. Borglum's publicity stunt worked well enough to get the state to build a road out to Mount Rushmore from Rapid City. Enough money also came in to keep work going through the summer season. As news of the project spread,

Opposite:
The 60-foot face of George Washington begins to emerge from the granite in 1930. Borglum was fond of saying that the faces of the presidents had always been there, they just needed to be brought into view by removing the unnecessary rock.

Top:
A rare photo,
taken in 1933,
shows the
original position
for Jefferson.

Bottom:
The Jefferson
head in
progress, in
its final
position, 1936.

visitors began to come to the site on a more regular basis.

The Washington head was mostly completed in 1941. Borglum, however, had originally planned to show the presidents from the waist up. When they began to carve Washington's coat and found that the granite changed lower on the mountain, the waist-length idea was abandoned and only the heads of the four presidents were done.

Originally, the Jefferson head was going to be on Washington's right, with Lincoln and Roosevelt to the left. Ninety feet of rock was removed on Washington's right in an effort to find stone solid enough to carve. The granite to Washington's right, however, was just not sound. In 1934, after $10,000 in labor and materials had been spent on Jefferson, the entire head had to be blasted away. Part of the problem had been that Borglum could not really tell what the rock would be like until it was actually carved. Another part of the problem was Borglum's initial stubborn insistence that the rock was suitable despite the many others who told him it was not. In the end, it was an argument that Mount Rushmore won: Jefferson had to be moved to Washington's left side.

The repositioning of the Jefferson head made Washington stand out more, but this new configuration was not without problems as well. When carving began on Jefferson's nose, a crack was discovered that might have eventually led to the nose breaking off over the years. Borglum had his workers reposition the head, tilting it back and to the right. The crack now runs from the right eye down through the chin, where it poses no problem. The only patch on the entire sculpture, made during the original carving, was on Jefferson. There, a foot-long piece of granite had to be patched in. Luigi Del Bianco was the stonecutter who made the patch, which is still hard to see even today.

As worked progressed on Lincoln, and started on Theodore Roosevelt, the Jefferson head was dedicated on August 30, 1936. The Jefferson dedication marked the halfway point in the completion of the memorial. President Franklin D. Roosevelt was there for the proceedings and hadn't planned to make a speech. But during the ceremony Borglum stood next to the president's car and spontaneously handed Roosevelt the microphone.

Sculptor Borglum (right) points out some details to President Franklin Roosevelt (middle) and Governor Tom Berry (left) at the dedication of the Jefferson head in 1936.

By 1936, both the Washington and Jefferson heads were mostly complete and the memorial was half finished.

1936 was one of the most productive years for the project, but it was also filled with problems. Borglum was having difficulty finding a suitable spot for Teddy Roosevelt's head. He had changed the model numerous times before he decided to put him between Lincoln and Jefferson. Once that decision was made, however, the problems were not over. Some of the worst rock of the project was in the area between Lincoln and Jefferson. Workers had to blast away 120 feet of stone before they found granite solid enough to begin carving. Borglum pressed on and, by the end of the 1936 work season, was within five feet of where Roosevelt's nose would eventually be.

During this time, the management of the project had switched from the commission to the National Park Service. For the most part, Borglum and his workers thought this was a positive change, as the Park Service did a lot of work upgrading the area and the equipment that was being used. Borglum, however, had problems dealing with the increased supervision. He was now required to follow federal hiring guidelines, and he reportedly went into a rage when the Park Service told him how much work they expected him to complete during the 1937 season.

In honor of the 150th anniversary of the Constitution, the Lincoln head was dedicated on September 17, 1937, in front of the 5,000 spectators that were in attendance. By this time, the popularity of the Mount Rushmore project was growing, and over 265,000 tourists visited the memorial that year. During this period, Borglum was away from Mount Rushmore much of the time, but he sent detailed instructions to

his son, Lincoln Borglum, who now worked as the official foreman at the site.

Lincoln had been with his father on the original scouting trip in the Black Hills and had been part of the crew every summer. He had worked without pay at first, and then was put on the payroll. As the sculptor's son, he had worked on every aspect of the sculpture. With his father away so much, Lincoln became the job's manager in 1937, and continued in that role until the end of the project.

Top: Work proceeds on the Lincoln head. ***Bottom:*** Borglum designed the eyes of his subjects with a raised area in the middle. This area catches the sunlight and makes the eyes appear to twinkle.

In 1938, Congress once again came to the rescue of Mount Rushmore by setting up yet another commission and giving $300,000 to the project. With adequate money available, Lincoln Borglum kept the crews working through the winter months. They only stopped for three weeks when it was just too cold to work. As long as the temperature was above -20 degrees Fahrenheit, the work went on. To keep the workers warm, tarps were hung on the scaffolding and fires were built in steel barrels placed at the back of the scaffolding.

Throughout the project, Gutzon Borglum received a twenty-five percent commission on the money spent carving Mount Rushmore. During 1938, his commission came to just over $16,000. The members of Congress who provided the money for the memorial were only making $10,000 that year.

The Hall of Records

One aspect of the project on which Borglum did not get his way had to do with the memorial's Hall of Records. The sculptor wanted this to be dug into the canyon wall behind the four heads, 80 feet deep, 60 feet wide, and 32 feet high. Inside the cave there were to be 25 statues of important Americans, such as Ben Franklin and Susan B. Anthony, and a number of scrolls describing what Borglum considered to be America's important achievements. Although work was started on the project, the Park Service and the new commission appointed by President Franklin D. Roosevelt forced Borglum to concentrate on completing the four presidents. Because of this order, the Hall of Records was never finished.

The entrance to the planned Hall of Records was located behind the carved figures. Construction began in 1939 but was never completed.

WHO CARVED MOUNT RUSHMORE?

Gutzon Borglum was the artist in charge of creating and overseeing the Mount Rushmore National Memorial. But 400 people did the actual work on the memorial, which took over 14 years to complete. For the most part, the workers

The work crew assembles for a group portrait in 1941. Lincoln Borglum is standing, far right in the second row.

were from the South Dakota area. Some were ranchers, others were loggers, and still others were miners. Whoever they were, they were glad to find work during the years of the Great Depression, when one out of four workers around the country was jobless.

Working for Borglum was not very easy: One of the carvers was fired and rehired eight times. The work was also demanding. The workday would begin at 7:30 A.M. and the workers would have a half hour to get up the stairway to the top and be ready to start at 8:00 A.M. After four hours, they would stop for lunch, and would then work until 4:00 P.M. Work on the memorial was relatively safe and there were only a few minor accidents. One was a freak accident that occurred when charges were being set during an electrical storm in the area. Lightning set off some of the blasting caps that a worker was handling.

Silicosis was probably the most serious health concern for the workers at Mount Rushmore. Most of them, though, were not even aware of its danger. Silicosis is caused by fine particles of rock dust that get into the lungs. The workers were all issued safety goggles and respirators but no one wore them. Long after the memorial was completed, at least two of the workers died from silicosis. Others were diagnosed with the condition.

About 30 men worked on the mountain at the same time. There would be pointers, who marked the rock to be removed; winchmen to work the winches that raised and lowered the workers on the sculpture; a "steel monkey" to bring sharpened bits to the drillers; call boys to communicate between the drillers and the winchmen; drillers (who were the most numerous); and powder monkeys who placed the dynamite charges and did the blasting. Many of the miners who did the drilling and blasting at Mount Rushmore had learned their trades in the nearby Holy Terror Gold Mine, which had shut down before the Rushmore project began.

When the memorial was first started, drillers got 50 cents to 60 cents per hour. Experienced stone carvers got as much as $1 per hour. Towards the end of the project, the hourly rates had gone up about 25 cents per hour for everyone.

Although the workers took their jobs seriously, they also found time to have some fun. In 1939, the Mount Rushmore baseball team reached the South Dakota state championships. At least one worker, Orville Worman, claimed he was hired as a driller simply because he was able to play shortstop.

The Finishing Touches

Gutzon Borglum's great project ran out of money again in February 1939. This time, when Congress came to the rescue with an additional $250,000, they set a deadline of June 1940 for completion of the memorial. By now, Borglum was 72 years old and in failing health, having expended much of his remaining energy arguing with the Park Service. Lincoln Borglum continued to do as much work as he could, but needed his father's input on the final artistic details of the huge carvings.

Opposite:
Theodore Roosevelt, set between Jefferson and Lincoln, was the last of the four heads to be completed.

33

By 1941, the memorial was near completion and only required final detailing, smoothing, and other finish work.

On July 2, 1939, Theodore Roosevelt's head was dedicated in front of a crowd of 12,000 people. The dedication was held at night with the mountain lit only by moonlight, as the ceremony started. The sculpture was then illuminated by fireworks exploding overhead, and, after the fireworks, searchlights

were used to light up Teddy Roosevelt and the other three presidents. The rest of that year, and through the 1940 season, as much final detailing as possible was done. But there was still more to do. Congress gave in on their original deadline and supplied another $86,000 for the 1941 season.

The End of an Era

In early March 1941, Gutzon Borglum was in Chicago for an appearance on a radio show when he became ill. He underwent emergency surgery, but died on March 6, 1941, from complications of the procedure. As the time to once again start work at Mount Rushmore approached, the commission asked Lincoln Borglum to become the sculptor in charge of the project and to do as much finishing up as he could during the 1941 season.

Lincoln once again brought up the Hall of Records idea, but got no further with it than his father had. Over the summer, Lincoln and his crew blocked out Jefferson's collar, reworked Washington's jaw, smoothed out Roosevelt's face, and finished Lincoln's beard. All the tools, air-lines, scaffolding, and other equipment used by the workers were then dismantled and put in storage. The 300-foot-high pile of rocks at the base of the mountain was left there as a reminder of work unfinished. Today, there are pine trees growing up out of the granite rubble.

By the fall of 1941, all work on Mount Rushmore had come to a halt, 14 years after it had begun. At that time, the National Park Service took over all aspects of managing the memorial, as it continues to do today.

A Memorial
for Millions

Over the years, the Park Service has worked hard to upgrade the facilities for visitors at Mount Rushmore. Parking lots have been expanded, Borglum's studio has become a museum, and an amphitheater has been built. A visitor center has also been constructed, along with a concession building, a viewing terrace, trails, and even lights so the memorial can be viewed at night. Despite the improvements, the facilities are still overcrowded: Over 2.5 million visitors a year come to Mount Rushmore. Approximately 1.7 million of those visitors come during the summer months of June, July, and August alone!

Opposite:
The 60-foot heads of the four presidents offer a dramatic view to visitors as the sunlight of the afternoon grows dim.

37

THE MODERN SIOUX

According to the 1990 U.S. census, there are over 103,000 Sioux across the country, almost 45,000 of which live in South Dakota. Approximately half of the Sioux in South Dakota live on the Pine Ridge Indian Reservation, which is not far from the Black Hills and Mount Rushmore. It was from the ancestors of the Sioux on Pine Ridge that the Black Hills was illegally taken in 1877. In an attempt to recover their lost lands, the Sioux went to court in 1923 to either get the Black Hills back or to receive another kind of compensation for their loss.

The case was dragged on in the courts for almost 60 years, during which time there were a number of demonstrations at Mount Rushmore, especially in the early 1970s. Many members of the American Indian Movement (AIM) spent two summers camped out at Mount Rushmore, regularly demonstrating at or near the memorial. Most Sioux then and now wanted the Black Hills—the center of their sacred world—returned. In 1980, when the U.S. Supreme Court finally handed down a decision in the case, it awarded the tribe $17.5 million plus five percent interest on the money since 1877. The Sioux have refused to take the money, in hopes of still getting their land back. The money is being held in trust and, with its accumulated interest, now totals over $250 million.

South Dakota Sioux perform during a modern-day powwow.

A scale model of the planned Crazy Horse memorial stands in front of the actual mountain, about three-quarters of a mile in the distance.

Crazy Horse Memorial

At least one person did something about the fact that Mount Rushmore did nothing to honor the Native Americans. Sioux Chief Henry Standing Bear asked the sculptor, Korczak Ziolkowski, if he could "Carve us a mountain so the white man will know that the red man had great heroes, too."

Ziolkowski was a well-known sculptor, whose work had taken first prize at the 1939 New York World's Fair. He was also a great admirer of Gutzon Borglum and Mount Rushmore. Ziolkowski and Henry Standing Bear traveled around the Black Hills looking for another mountain that could be carved up, but their search was interrupted by World War II (1941-1945). After the war, Ziolkowski returned to South Dakota and spent most of his personal savings to buy Thunderhead Mountain,

located about 90 miles from Pine Ridge, South Dakota.

Ziolkowski decided the subject of this sculpture would be the famous Sioux leader, Crazy Horse. In 1947, he moved his family from Connecticut to Thunderhead Mountain. His plans called for a three-dimensional sculpture of Crazy Horse mounted on a horse that would be 641 feet long and 563 feet high when complete.

Ziolkowski died in 1982, but eight of his ten children and his wife Ruth continue to live at, and work on, the Crazy Horse Memorial. Today, visitors to Thunderhead Mountain can see the rough outline of the sculpture taking form. Someday, Native Americans may have this sculpture as a memorial that speaks both to their triumphs and defeats throughout history as important participants in the building of America.

Mount Rushmore hosts more than 2.5 million people a year, with over half of the visitors arriving during June, July, and August.

Even more important than providing services for Mount Rushmore's visitors, the Park Service must continually inspect and maintain the actual sculpture. Each year, a team of maintenance workers uses Borglum's original system of winches and cables to lower themselves onto the faces of the four presidents in order to clean and care for them. The most important aspect of this process is the filling of any new cracks. The cracks are only a problem if they are allowed to fill with water during the winter, since the water freezes and then expands. Expansion of water inside the cracks can break off pieces of rock. To prevent this, all cracks are filled with a special silicone mixture manufactured by Dow Corning.

Keeping up with technology, the Park Service has authorized a series of computer-aided analyses of Mount Rushmore to answer certain questions of position and stability. Although not complete, the initial results indicate that the sculpture will be there for many, many years to come. In doing these analyses, 99 bulls-eye-like markers were placed on the sculpture and the mountain. Photos were also taken from a variety of angles, including from the air. The photos were then used to feed information into a computer where a CAD (computer-aided design) program provided useful planning and maintenance information to the Park Service.

Fiftieth Anniversary Party

On July 3, 1991, a spectacular event, attended by President George Bush and a number of other celebrities, was held at Mount Rushmore to celebrate the memorial's fiftieth anniversary. Among the many special events, Radio City Music Hall put on a production that dramatized the carving of the memorial. The celebration's most honored guests, however, were 19 of Borglum's original workers.

The Mount Rushmore Memorial Society also used the celebration to kick off a major fundraising drive. It is their plan to raise $40 million to improve the visitor facilities and repair and maintain the memorial so that it may remain a "shrine to democracy" for many years to come. Certainly, Mount Rushmore will forever remain not only a memorial to the strength of our great nation, but also a permanent reminder of the spirit and vision of a man named Gutzon Borglum.

Today, Mount Rushmore stands
not only as a tribute to four of
America's greatest leaders, but
also as a memorial to the talent
and dedication of its sculptor,
Gutzon Borglum.

GLOSSARY

blasting cap A small explosive device that is used to detonate dynamite.

bumper A small air-powered hammer that was used to smooth the surface of the sculpture.

call boy A worker who relayed instructions from workers on the sculpture to the winch operators on top.

chisel A hard metal tool that is struck with a hammer to remove small quantities of stone.

Confederacy The southern states that separated from the United States and fought against the northern states in the Civil War.

driller A worker who operates an air-powered stone drill.

dynamite A powerful explosive used to remove stone or other material from a work site.

foreman A worker who supervises a group of other workers.

hard-rock mining The removal of valuable minerals from solid rock.

honeycombing The removal of rock by drilling a large number of closely spaced holes and then removing the rock between the holes.

jackhammer An air-powered hammer that comes in a variety of sizes: Jackhammers weighing from 25 to 60 pounds were used at Mount Rushmore. Some jackhammers are used for drilling while others move in and out and are used like hammers.

magma The hot, liquid, inner core of the earth that occasionally flows out onto the earth's surface in the form of lava.

outcropping A geological term used to describe a formation that stands out from the surrounding landscape.

plumb bob A weight that is tied to the end of a cord to create a straight vertical line.

pointer A worker who took measurements from the models and transferred them to points on the mountainside.

powder monkey The name given to workers who are responsible for placing and detonating the dynamite charges.

scaffolding A temporary platform for workers to stand on when working above ground level.

sectional mold A molded re-creation of Borglum's studio models of the presidents' heads.

silicosis A serious disease caused by the accumulation of rock dust in the lungs.

steel monkey The worker who is responsible for keeping the drillers supplied with sharp bits for their drills.

stonecutter A worker who is experienced in the finishing and cutting of stone for artistic and architectural purposes.

tarp A large, heavy, waterproof piece of cloth used to protect workers or a project from the weather.

temper To harden metal through the use of heat.

winch A mechanical device that winds a rope or cable up or down.

winchman A worker responsible for cranking other workers up and down the mountain.

CHRONOLOGY

1867 March 25—Gutzon Borglum born.

1874 Gold is discovered in the Black Hills of South Dakota.

1875 President Grant declares war on the Sioux.

1876 Custer is defeated at the Battle of the Little Big Horn.

Army retaliates and crushes the Sioux nation.

Pine Ridge Reservation is established and most Sioux sent there.

1923 Sioux bring suit in federal court to get the Black Hills back.

1924 Doane Robinson, South Dakota state historian, contacts Gutzon Borglum about creating a massive sculpture in the Black Hills.

1925 August—Borglum and his son, Lincoln, visit Black Hills and choose Mount Rushmore as site for a memorial.

1927 March 27—Borglum signs an agreement with the Mount Harney Association to carve a memorial at Mount Rushmore.

August 10—First drilling ceremony is held.

October 4—Work starts on the mountain.

1929 Public Law 805 is passed by U.S. Congress, which authorizes matching federal funds for Mount Rushmore project.

1930 July 4—Washington head dedicated.

Crew works from August 15 to November 6.

1931 Crew works from June 5 to October 1.

1932 No work done, project out of money.

1933 Congress authorizes additional money.

March 24—Work season starts.

1934 Jefferson head blasted off and restarted in a new location.

1935 Crews worked from June to November.

1936 August 30—Jefferson head is dedicated.

1937 September 17—Lincoln head is dedicated.

1938 Congress authorizes $300,000 and crews work through the winter.

1939 Congress authorizes another $250,000 and gives project deadline of June.

1940 July 2—Roosevelt head dedicated.

Congress grants another $86,000 for finish work during 1941.

1941 March 6—Gutzon Borglum dies in Chicago.

Lincoln Borglum is appointed sculptor in charge and asked to complete work.

October 31—Last day of work on the Mount Rushmore National Memorial.

1972 First of a series of American Indian Movement (AIM) demonstrations at Mount Rushmore.

1980 Sioux win Black Hills suit and are awarded $17.5 million plus five percent interest for lands illegally taken from them in 1877.

1991 Fiftieth anniversary celebration held at Mount Rushmore.

Fundraising drive is started to raise $40 million for the improvement and preservation of Mount Rushmore.

FURTHER READING

Ayer, Eleanor. *Our National Memorials.* Brookfield, CT: Millbrook Press, 1992.

Goodson, Rose Mary. *The Rushmore Story—Why the Mountain Memorial.* Piedmont, SD: Rose Mary Goodson Publishing, 1982.

Lepthien, Emilie. *South Dakota.* Chicago: Childrens Press, 1991.

Marsh, Carole. *South Dakota Jeopardy! Questions and Answers About Our State.* Decatur, GA: Gallopade Publishing, 1991.

Pekarik, Andrew. *Sculpture.* New York: Hyperion, 1992.

St. George, Judith. *The Mount Rushmore Story.* New York: G.P. Putnam's Sons, 1985.

SOURCE NOTES

Bartruff, Dave. "The Men Who Mend Mountains." *World* +1, v 6 n 7, July 1, 1991, 438.

Boime, Albert. "Patriarchy Fixed in Stone." *American Art*, Winter 1991, 143-167.

Chu, Daniel, and Shaw, Bill. "About Faces." *People*, July 22, 1991, 69-70.

"Does Mount Rushmore Need a Facelift?" *Science News*, November 17, 1990, 319.

Dowd, Maureen. "For Bush, a Special Day at Mount Rushmore." *NY Times*, July 4, 1991, A-8.

Hadley, C. J. "To the Badlands and Beyond." *Saturday Evening Post*, July/August 1990, 82-90.

Heard, Alex. "Mount Rushmore: The Real Story." *New Republic*, July 15 & 22, 1991, 16-18.

Jackson, Donald Dale. "Gutzon Borglum's Odd and Awesome Portraits in Granite." *Smithsonian*, v 23 n 5, August 1992, 64-75.

Mount Rushmore National Memorial. Second Book. Mount Rushmore National Memorial Commission, 1931.

Nassar, Jennifer. "Carved for the Ages." *Americana*, June 1991, 52-53.

Shaff, Howard, and Shaff, Audrey Karl. *Six Wars at a Time: The Life and Times of Gutzon Borglum, Sculptor of Mount Rushmore.* Sioux Falls, SD: Center for Western Studies, 1985.

St. George, Judith. *The Mount Rushmore Story.* New York: Putnam's, 1985.

Vogt, Tim, and Smith, Denise J. "Presenting the Vision." *Cadence.* October 1991, 32-35.

INDEX

American Indian Movement
   (AIM), 38
Anthony, Susan B., 30

Bear, Henry Standing, 39
Black Hills, 5, 8, 29, 39
   and Sioux, 14, 38
Borglum, Gutzon, 13, 15, 19, 22, 25,
   31, 33, 39, 40, 41
   about, 10–11
   commission, 30
   death of, 35
   models, 17–18, 28
   planning sculpture, 5, 7–9, 12
   work on sculpture, 23, 26, 27, 29
Borglum, James Lincoln, 5, 11, 29,
   30, 33, 35
Borglum, Jens, 10
Borglum, Mary Ellis, 11
Bridger, James, 9
Bush, George, 41

Civil War, 12
Coolidge, Calvin, 13, 15, 22
Crazy Horse, 39
Crazy Horse Memorial, 39

Del Bianco, Luigi, 27

Franklin, Ben, 30
Fremont, John, 9

Great Depression, 15, 31

Hall of Records, 30, 35

Jefferson, Thomas (head), 5, 28
   dedication, 27

selection, 9
work on, 26–27, 35

Kennedy, John F., 12

Lewis and Clark, 9
Lincoln, Abraham (head), 5, 26, 28
   dedication, 29
   selection, 9, 12
   work on, 27, 35
Little Big Horn, 14
Louisiana Purchase, 9

Mikkelson, Christina, 10
Mikkelson, Ida, 10
Montgomery, Mary, 10
Mount Rushmore
   controversy, 5, 7–8, 9, 12
   dedication, 13
   fiftieth anniversary, 41
   financing, 12–13, 15, 25, 30, 33,
   35, 41
   laws and, 15, 22
   maintaining, 40–41
   models for, 17–18
   tools used on, 19–23, 35, 40
   visitors to, 26, 29, 34, 37, 40
   workers, 18–19, 20–23, 31, 41
Mount Rushmore Memorial
   National Commission, 15, 28, 30,
   35
Mount Rushmore Memorial Society,
   41

National Environmental Policy Act, 22
National Park Service, 28–29, 30, 33,
   35, 37, 40, 41
Norbeck, Peter, 15

Panama Canal, 12
Pine Ridge Reservation, 38
Presley, Elvis, 12
Putnam, Lisa, 10

Robinson, Doane, 5, 7, 8, 9, 12
Rodin, Auguste, 10
Roosevelt, Franklin D., 15, 27, 30
Roosevelt, Theodore (head), 5, 26
　　dedication, 34
　　selection, 12
　　work on, 27, 28, 35

Shoemaker, Theodore, 8
Silicosis, 31
Sioux, 14, 38

South Dakota Historical Society, 5
Stone Mountain project, 5, 11, 13,
　19

Thunderhead Mountain, 39

Washington, George (head), 5
　　dedication, 25
　　selection, 9
　　work on, 25, 26, 35
Williamson, William, 15
World War II, 39
Worman, Orville, 31

Ziolkowski, Korczak, 39